Piano ~ Vocal ~ Guitar

CHART HITS OF '94 '5

ISBN 0-7935-4377-0

HAL•LEONARD™
CORPORATION
7777 W. BLUEMOUND RD. P.O. BOX 13819 MILWAUKEE, WI 53213

CONTENTS

100% PURE LOVE

Words and Music by CRYSTAL WATERS, TEDDY DOUGLAS,
JAY STEINHOUR and TOMMY DAVIS

take you there, show you how to care. ___ Just
name a - gain. No, it's not a sin. ___ I'll show you

be a - ware ___ that you'll have to share. I want your love. I want it to -
how to win ___ and where I've been.

night. ___ I'm tak - ing your heart ___ so, don't you

Am

Gm **Am** **Gm7** **Am**

Gm9 **Gm** **Am**

fight. ___ I'll be your an - swer, ___ I'll be your

ALWAYS

Words and Music by
JON BON JOVI

This Ro - me - o is bleed - ing,
pic - tures that you left be - hind are just

Well, there ain't no luck ___ in these

when I die ___ you'll be on my mind ___ and I'll love you,

al - ways.

Guitar solo - ad lib. and Fade

Repeat ad lib. and Fade

Lead vocal ad lib.

ALWAYS IN MY HEART

Words and Music by BABYFACE
and DARYL SIMMONS

ANYTIME YOU NEED A FRIEND

Words and Music by MARIAH CAREY
and WALTER AFANASIEFF

If you're lone - ly
When the sha - dows
and need a friend ___
are clos - ing in ___

and trou - bles seem ___ like
and your spir - it
they nev - er end, ___
dim - in - ish - ing, ___

just re - mem - ber
just re - mem - ber
to keep the faith ___
you're not a - lone ___

AT YOUR BEST (YOU ARE LOVE)

Words and Music by O'KELLY ISLEY, RONALD ISLEY,
RUDOLPH ISLEY, ERNIE ISLEY, MARVIN ISLEY and CHRIS JASPER

BEAUTIFUL IN MY EYES

Words and Music by
JOSHUA KADISON

BUT IT'S ALRIGHT

Words and Music by JEROME L. JACKSON
and PIERRE TUBBS

You don't know   how   I   feel. ___   You'll
One ___ day   you'll   see ___   you'll
There's one thing   I   wan - na say,   you'll

nev - er   know _____   how   I   feel. ___
nev - er   find _____   a   guy   like   me
meet   a   guy _____   who'll   make   you   pay,

CIRCLE OF LIFE

Music by ELTON JOHN
Lyrics by TIM RICE

OU FEEL THE LOVE TONIGHT

from Walt Disney Pictures' THE LION KING

Music by ELTON JOHN
Lyrics by TIM RICE

CRAZY

Words and Music by STEVEN TYLER,
JOE PERRY and DESMOND CHILD

(Spoken:) Come here, baby. You know you drive me up a wall with the way you make good on all the nasty tricks you pull. Seems like we're makin' up more than we're makin' love. And it always seems you got something on your mind other than me.

Slowly, with a steady beat

Girl, you got to change your crazy ways, you hear me?

Say you're leav-in' on a sev-en-thir-ty train and that you're
You're pack-in' up your stuff and talk-in' like it's tough and tryin' to

head-in' out to Hol-ly-wood.___ Girl, you been giv-in' me that line so man-y times it kind-a
tell me that it's time to go,___ but I know you ain't wear-in' noth-in' un-der-neath that o-ver-

gets like feel-in' bad looks good.___ That kind-a lov-in' turns a
coat, and it's all a show.___ That kind-a lov-in' makes me wan-na

CREEP

Words and Music by
DALLAS AUSTIN

ENDLESS LOVE

Words and Music by
LIONEL RICHIE

My love, there's on-ly you in my life,
Two hearts, two hearts that beat as one;

the on-ly thing that's right. My first love,
our lives have just be-gun. For-ev-er,

you're ev-'ry breath that I take, you're ev-'ry
I'll hold you close in my arms, I can't re-

DON'T TURN AROUND

Words and Music by DIANE WARREN
and ALBERT HAMMOND

FALL DOWN

Music by TODD NICHOLS, GLEN PHILLIPS and TOAD
Lyrics by GLEN PHILLIPS and TODD NICHOLS

When will we fall, when will we fall?

D.S. al Coda

CODA

I'LL MAKE LOVE TO YOU

Words and Music by
BABYFACE

Slowly, in a steady 2

Close your eyes, make a wish, and blow
lax, let's go slow. I ain't

HERO

Words and Music by MARIAH CAREY
and WALTER AFANASIEFF

HOUSE OF LOVE

Words and Music by WALLY WILSON,
KENNY GREENBERG and GREG BARNHILL

Well, I bet you an-y a-mount of mon-ey he'll be com-ing

back to you.___ Ooh, I know there ain't no doubt a-bout it. Some-times life is

I MISS YOU

Words by AARON HALL
Music by GREGORY CAUTHEN

I'LL REMEMBER

from the film WITH HONORS

Words and Music by RICHARD PAGE,
PAT LEONARD and MADONNA CICCONE

I'M READY

Words and Music by
BABYFACE

LIVING IN DANGER

Words and Music by
buddha and joker

(Spoken:) Live for yourself, it's a wonderful thing. You can do what you want, you can live in a dream.

Get up,   *get in,*   *get the rhythm,*   *get down.*   **You're**

LOVE IS ALL AROUND

Featured on the Motion Picture Soundtrack
FOUR WEDDINGS AND A FUNERAL

Words and Music by
REG PRESLEY

I feel it in my fin-gers, I feel it in my toes._
see your face be-fore me as I lay on my bed._

Love __ is all a-round me,
I kind-a get to think-ing

and so the feel-ing grows._ It's
of all the things you said, __ oh, yes I do. You

LOVE SNEAKIN' UP ON YOU

Words and Music by JIMMY SCOTT
and TOM SNOW

Rain-y night,— I'm all a-lone,—
No-where on earth — for your heart to hide —

sit-ting here wait-ing for your voice on the — phone. —
once love comes sneak-in' up on your blind _____ side, _____

up on you. _ Hey, _____ yeah.

up on you. _ Well, _____

LUCKY ONE

Words and Music by AMY GRANT
and KEITH THOMAS

You're the kind ___ when you
You're the kind ___ that I

ba - by, I'm the luck - y one. _____

MAYBE LOVE WILL CHANGE YOUR MIND

Words and Music by RICK NOWELS
and SANDY STEWART

MMM MMM MMM MMM

Words and Music by
BRAD ROBERTS

worse than __ that.

'Cause

THE POWER OF LOVE

Words by MARY SUSAN APPLEGATE and JENNIFER RUSH
Music by CANDY DEROUGE and GUNTHER MENDE

RETURN TO INNOCENCE

Words and Music by
CURLY M.C.

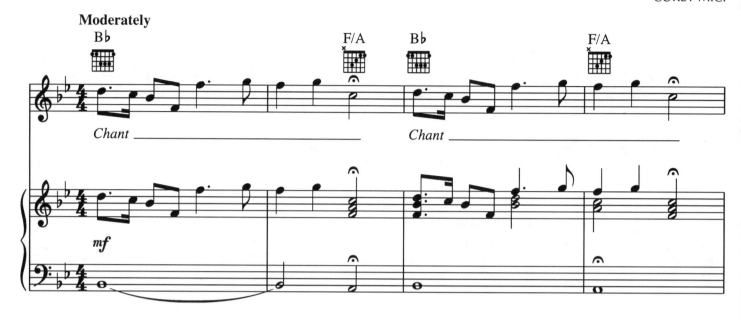

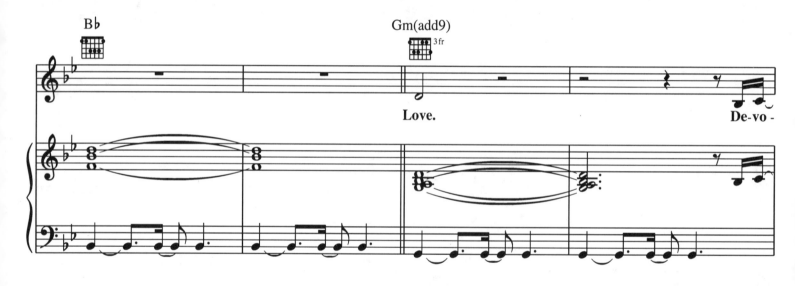

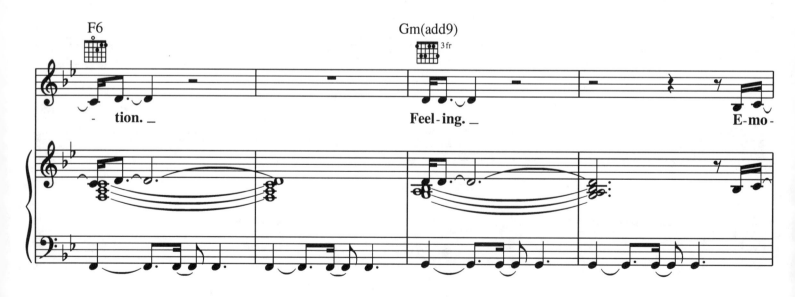

144

(Spoken:) That's not the beginning of the end. That's the return to yourself,

the return to innocence.

Instrumental solo (2 times)
Vocal chant ad lib. (5 times)

Play 7 times

(Spoken:) That's the return to innocence.

SUKIYAKI

Words and Music by HACHIDAI NAKAMURA
and ROKUSUKE EI

Moderately, not too fast

no chord

mf

It's all be-cause of you I'm feel-ing sad and blue.

You went a-way. Now my life is just a rain-y day.

And I love you so, how much you'll nev-er know.

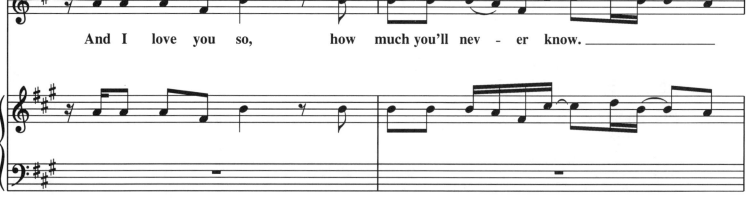

ROCK AND ROLL DREAMS COME THROUGH

Words and Music by
JIM STEINMAN

SECRET

Words and Music by DALLAS AUSTIN
and MADONNA CICCONE

THE SIGN

Words and Music by buddha, joker,
jenny and linn

(I,) I got a new _ life. You'd hard-ly rec-og-nize_ me. I'm_ so glad.
(I,) un-der the pale _ moon for so man-y years I won-dered who_ you are.

THE SWEETEST DAYS

Words and Music by JON LIND,
PHIL GALDSTON and WENDY WALDMAN

TAKE A BOW

Words and Music by BABYFACE
and MADONNA

Take a bow, ___ the night is o - ver. This
Make them laugh, ___ it comes so eas - y when you

WHAT'S THE FREQUENCY, KENNETH?

Words and Music by BILL BERRY, PETER BUCK,
MIKE MILLS and MICHAEL STIPE

"What's the fre-quen-cy, Ken -neth?" is your ben - ze - drine.
I'd stud-ied your car- toons, ra - di - o, mu - sic, t v, mov-ies,mag - a - zines.
"What's the fre-quen-cy, Ken-neth?" is your ben - ze - drine.

Guitar solo-ad lib.

Solo ends

D.S. al Coda

CODA

You wore a shirt___ of vi - o - lent green.
You wore our ex - pec - ta - tions like an ar - mored suit.
You wore a shirt___ of vi - o - lent green.

I could-n't un-der-stand.
I could-n't un-der-stand.

I nev-er un-der-stood the fre-quen-cy,
You said that i - ro-ny was the shack-les of youth.
I nev-er un-der-stood, don't fuck with me.

THINKIN' PROBLEM

Words and Music by STUART ZIFF,
DAVID BALL and ALLEN SHAMBLIN

Yes, I ad - mit I got a think-in' prob - lem.

She's al-ways on __ my mind. ___ Her mem - 'ry goes

round and round. __ I've tried to quit __ a thou - sand

I keep on ___ re-

I'll start ____ with lov - in' her, _____

but I don't know when _ to stop.

TURN THE BEAT AROUND

from the Motion Picture THE SPECIALIST

Words and Music by PETER JACKSON JR.
and GERALD JACKSON

WHEN CAN I SEE YOU

Words and Music by
BABYFACE

Moderately (not too fast)

Lyrics:

When can my heart beat a - gain?____
When does my some - day be - gin ____

When does the pain ev - er end?____
when I'll find some - one a - gain?____

And when do the tears stop from run - ning o - ver?____
And what if I still am not tru - ly o - ver?____

WHEN WE DANCE

Words and Music by
STING

Repeat and Fade

YOU GOTTA BE

Words and Music by DES'REE
Additional Music by ASHLEY INGRAM

Lis-ten as __ your day __ un-folds, __ chal-lenge what __ the fu-ture holds. __

YOU MEAN THE WORLD TO ME

Words and Music by BABYFACE,
L.A. REID and DARYL SIMMONS

Contemporary Classics

Your *favorite songs for piano, voice and guitar.*

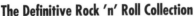

The Definitive Rock 'n' Roll Collection

A classic collection of the best songs from the early rock 'n' roll years – 1955-1966. 97 songs, including: Barbara Ann • Chantilly Lace • Dream Lover • Duke Of Earl • Earth Angel • Great Balls Of Fire • Louie, Louie • Rock Around The Clock • Ruby Baby • Runaway • (Seven Little Girls) Sitting In The Back Seat • Stay • Surfin' U.S.A. • Wild Thing • Woolly Bully • and more.

00490195 ....$22.95

The Big Book Of Rock

78 of rock's biggest hits, including: Addicted To Love • American Pie • Born To Be Wild • Cold As Ice • Dust In The Wind • Free Bird • Goodbye Yellow Brick Road • Groovin' • Hey Jude • I Love Rock N Roll • Lay Down Sally • Layla • Livin' On A Prayer • Louie Louie • Maggie May • Me And Bobby McGee • Monday, Monday • Owner Of A Lonely Heart • Shout • Walk This Way • We Didn't Start The Fire • You Really Got Me • and more.

00311566..$19.95

Big Book Of Movie And TV Themes

Over 90 familiar themes, including: Alfred Hitchcock Theme • Beauty And The Beast • Candle On The Water • Theme From *E.T.* • Endless Love • Hawaii Five-O • I Love Lucy • Theme From *Jaws* • Jetsons • Major Dad Theme • The Masterpiece • Mickey Mouse March • The Munsters Theme • Theme From *Murder, She Wrote* • Mystery • Somewhere Out There • Unchained Melody • Won't You Be My Neighbor • and more!

00311582 ....$19.95

The Best Rock Songs Ever

70 of the best rock songs from yesterday and today, including: All Day And All Of The Night • All Shook Up • Ballroom Blitz • Bennie And The Jets • Blue Suede Shoes • Born To Be Wild • Boys Are Back In Town • Every Breath You Take • Faith • Free Bird • Hey Jude • I Still Haven't Found What I'm Looking For • Livin' On A Prayer • Lola • Louie Louie • Maggie May • Money • (She's) Some Kind Of Wonderful • Takin' Care Of Business • Walk This Way • We Didn't Start The Fire • We Got The Beat • Wild Thing • more!

00490424 ....$16.95

#1 Songs Of The 90's

Over 20 of today's top chartburning hits, including: Baby Baby • Emotions • Gonna Make You Sweat • How Am I Supposed To Live Without You • Vision Of Love • You're In Love • and more.

00311584 ....$12.95

35 Classic Hits

35 contemporary favorites, including: Beauty And The Beast • Dust In The Wind • Just The Way You Are • Moon River • The River Of Dreams • Somewhere Out There • Tears In Heaven • When I Fall In Love • A Whole New World (Aladdin's Theme) • and more.

00311654 ....$12.95

55 Contemporary Standards

55 favorites, including: Alfie • Beauty And The Beast • Can't Help Falling In Love • Candle In The Wind • Have I Told You Lately • How Am I Supposed To Live Without You • Memory • The River Of Dreams • Sea Of Love • Tears In Heaven • Up Where We Belong • When I Fall In Love • and more.

00311670 ....$15.95

The New Grammy® Awards Song Of The Year Songbook

Every song named Grammy Awards' "Song Of The Year" from 1958 to 1988. 28 songs, featuring: Volare • Moon River • The Shadow Of Your Smile • Up, Up and Away • Bridge Over Troubled Water • You've Got A Friend • Killing Me Softly With His Song • The Way We Were • You Light Up My Life • Evergreen • Sailing • Bette Davis Eyes • We Are The World • That's What Friends Are For • Somewhere Out There • Don't Worry, Be Happy.

00359932 ....$12.95

Soft Rock – Revised

39 romantic mellow hits, including: Beauty And The Beast • Don't Know Much • Save The Best For Last • Vision Of Love • Just Once • Dust In The Wind • Just The Way You Are • Your Song.

00311596 ....$14.95

37 Super Hits Of The Superstars

37 big hits by today's most popular artists, including Billy Joel, Amy Grant, Elton John, Rod Stewart, Mariah Carey, Wilson Phillips, Paula Abdul and many more. Songs include: Addicted To Love • Baby Baby • Endless Love • Here And Now • Hold On • Lost In Your Eyes • Love Takes Time • Vision Of Love • We Didn't Start The Fire.

00311539 ....$14.95

Prices, contents & availability subject to change without notice.